The Secret Room

"Each of you should look not only
to your own interests,
but also to the interests of others."
Philippians 2:4

The Standard Publishing Company, Cincinnati, Ohio
A division of Standex International Corporation
© 1994 by The Standard Publishing Company
All rights reserved.
Printed in the United States of America.
01 00 99 98 97 96 95 94   5 4 3 2 1

ISBN 8-7847-0179-2
Cataloging-in-Publication data available

Edited by Diane Stortz
Designed by Coleen Davis

Contents

The Shopping Spree

Troy Foxworth looked

in the window

of Uncle Dudley's Toy Store.

"Race cars!" said Troy.

"Model airplanes!

Baseball gloves!

And Tough Ted's Power Tank!

This is great!" Troy went inside.

Lights flashed.

Buzzers buzzed.

"Surprise!" said Uncle Dudley.

"You are the one hundredth
customer in my new store!
And you win
a five-minute shopping spree!
On your mark, get set, go!"

Troy raced through the store.

"Race cars!" said Troy.

"Model airplanes!

Baseball gloves!

And Tough Ted's Power Tank!

This is great!"

When five minutes were up,

lights flashed and buzzers buzzed.

"Great job!" said Uncle Dudley.

"Everything in your cart is free."

"Thanks, Uncle Dudley," said Troy.

"Thanks a lot!"

Troy pushed the cart full of toys
up to his front door.

"Mom!" called Troy.

"Dad! Where are you!"

No one answered.

Troy found his mother

digging in her garden.

"Mom!" said Troy. "Guess what!

I won a shopping spree

at Uncle Dudley's Toy Store."

"Good for you, Troy,"

said Mrs. Foxworth.

"Now let me finish the garden."

Mr. Foxworth had supper
cooking on the grill.

"Guess what, Dad!" said Troy.

"I won a shopping spree
at Uncle Dudley's Toy Store."

"Good for you, Troy,"
said Mr. Foxworth.

"Now let me
finish
cooking
supper."

Troy found his brother, Warren,

watching TV in his room.

"Guess what, Warren!" said Troy.

"I won a shopping spree

at Uncle Dudley's Toy Store."

"Later, Troy," said Warren.

"I'm trying to watch the game."

Troy looked in his sister's room.

"Guess what, Vixen!" said Troy.

"I won a shopping spree
at Uncle Dudley's Toy Store."

"Later, Troy," said Vixen.

"I'm painting
a picture."

Troy went to his room

and lay on his bed.

"No one cares about my prize,"

he said to Tough Ted.

"Everyone is too busy."

15

The Hidden Door

Troy rolled Tough
Ted's Power Tank down the path
beside the foxhole.
His prizes did not seem as
wonderful as they had at first.

16

"I wish everyone
wasn't so busy," Troy said.
He put Tough Ted
in the Power Tank
and pushed it down the path.

CRASH!

The Power Tank hit a branch.

Tough Ted fell out.

He disappeared into the vines

that covered the hill.

"I will find you, Tough Ted!"
said Troy. He lay on his stomach
and pushed aside some vines.

He could see Tough Ted
at the bottom of the hill.

Troy crawled down through the

vines to rescue Tough Ted.

"There you are!" said Troy.

"But what's this?"

Tough Ted was lying

beside the word

WELCOME.

"Who put this old doormat
down here in the vines?"
said Troy. Then he looked up.
He saw an old door
covered with vines.

21

Troy pulled the vines

away from the door.

The door opened just enough

for Troy to squeeze through.

"A secret room!" said Troy.

"Dad! Mom!" he shouted.

"Warren! Vixen! Come quick!

And bring a flashlight!"

The Secret Room

Troy's whole family

stood in the middle

of the secret room.

"Look," said Mr. Foxworth.

He pointed at the wall.

"It's a sealed up doorway,"

he said. "At one time this room

was part of the house."

"I wonder why it was sealed up," said Mrs. Foxworth.

"I don't know," said Troy.

"But I have an idea.

Let's turn this room

into *my* new bedroom!

I need more room for all my toys."

"*Your* bedroom?" said Warren.

"I should get it. I'm the oldest."

"I could turn

this room into my art studio,"

said Vixen. She waved her

paintbrush through the air.

26

"Sorry, kids," said Mr. Foxworth.
"I need this room to store the
grill and all my tools."

"Hold it," said Mrs. Foxworth.
"I want to put in windows
and fill this room
with beautiful plants."

Suddenly, everyone was yelling at everyone else.

And everyone except Troy stomped out of the secret room.

In a corner of the room,

Troy had seen a box.

What was in it?

Inside the dusty box,

Troy found a book.

He took it to his room.

The Photo Album

No one spoke during supper.

After supper,

Troy went back to his room

and opened the book

from the secret room.

He read the first page.

A book
about Me
by
Roxie
Redtail

Troy turned the pages.

"A photo album!" he said.

The pictures had been taken

a long time ago.

In the pictures was a girl

about Troy's age.

This is my family. Mother, Father, Cubby, Rusty, Hunter, me, and Grandma Silverfur.

Here I am on my first birthday. I love birthday cake!

I am the only girl in my family. I am also the youngest. I like to play with my brother.

My family spends many evenings after supper in the family room.

Troy looked closely at the picture

of the family room.

"It is the secret room!" he said.

But the room in the picture

looked warm and comfortable.

Now it was dark and cold.

There were more photos in the book.

this is Grandma Silverfur and me, quilting together.

Hunter is my oldest brother. He went to school to be a doctor.

Here is Rusty on his Wedding day. I was in the wedding.

Here is cubby.

He became a pilo,

only mother, father, and I live here now.

Here we are cleaning out the family room.

The last page

of the photo album said,

Father closed up
the family room.
We do not need
so much space now.
I will miss the
family room.

Troy closed the photo album.

He sat on his bed

for a long time.

Roxie Redtail's family

had a family room, thought Troy.

Maybe that is what

my family needs. A family room!

The Family Room

"Mom! Dad! Warren! Vixen!"

called Troy.

"Look what I found

in the secret room."

Everyone was still angry
with everyone else.
But one by one
the whole family came
to the kitchen table
to look at the photos.

"This photo album
has given me an idea," said Troy.
"What our family needs
is a family room.
Let's turn the secret room
back into a family room!"

One by one,
Mr. Foxworth

and Mrs. Foxworth

and Warren

and Vixen

began to smile

at each other and at Troy.

The next day,

Mr. Foxworth made an opening

from the kitchen

down to the family room.

Warren built some shelves.

Troy swept the floor.

Mrs. Foxworth cleaned the walls,

and Vixen put rugs on the floor.

Then Warren
moved his TV
into the new room.
Vixen hung
her paintings
on the walls.
Mrs. Foxworth
put out plants.
Troy put Tough Ted
and the Power Tank
on the new shelves.
And Mr. Foxworth
brought in snacks.

That night after supper,

Troy and his family

played games

in their new family room . . .

together!